THE
OTTOMAN
EMPIRE

To my father

With thanks to Indira Falk Gesink,
Professor of Middle Eastern History,
Baldwin Wallace College, Berea, Ohio,
for her thoughtful reading of the manuscript

CULTURES OF THE PAST

THE OTTOMAN EMPIRE

ADRIANE RUGGIERO

BENCHMARK BOOKS

MARSHALL CAVENDISH
NEW YORK

Benchmark Books
Marshall Cavendish
99 White Plains Road
Tarrytown, New York 10591-9001
www.marshallcavendish.com

Library of Congress Cataloging-in-Publication Data

Ruggiero, Adriane.
      The Ottoman Empire / by Adriane Ruggiero.
            p.   cm.— (Cultures of the past)
      Summary: Examines the history, culture, religion, society, and achievements of the Ottoman Empire, from its tribal origins in the 1200s to its decline in the early twentieth century.
      Includes bibliographical references and index.
      Contents: History: from nomads to sultans—Cultural history: the peak—The age of Suleyman the Magnificent—Belief system: the Turks and Islam—Beliefs and society: putting their stamp on the empire—The legacy of the Ottomans: a 600-year-old state whose influence lives on.
      ISBN 0-7614-1494-0
      1. Turkey—History—Ottoman Empire, 1288–1918—Juvenile literature. 2. Turkey—Social life and customs—Juvenile literature. [1. Turkey—History—Ottoman Empire, 1288–1918. 2. Turkey—Social life and customs.] I. Title. II. Series.
      DR485 .R84   2002
      956.1'015—dc21   2002002264

Printed in Hong Kong

Book design by Carol Matsuyama
Art research by Rose Corbett Gordon, Mystic CT

Front cover: Selling spices in the bazaar, a lithograph by Adolphe Jean-Baptiste Bayot (1810–1866)
Back cover: At Prayer in the Mosque, 1884, by Filipo Bartolini

Photo Credits

Front cover: Stapleton Collection, UK/Bridgeman Art Library; back cover: Victoria & Albert Museum, London/Bridgeman Art Library; pages 7, 43: Bibliotheque Nationale, Paris/Bridgeman Art; pages 9, 27, 65: Giraudon/Art Resource, NY; page 10: Topkapi Palace Museum, Istanbul/Bridgeman Art Library; pages 12, 23, 24: The Granger Collection, New York; page 14: Musée des Augustins, Toulouse, France/Bridgeman Art Library; pages 15, 55, 70–71: Stapleton Collection, UK/Bridgeman Art Library; page18: Palacio del Senado, Madrid/Bridgeman Art Library; page 21: Bibliotheque des Arts Decoratifs, Paris/Bridgeman Art Library; page 29: Nik Wheeler/Corbis; pages 30–31: The Art Archive; pages 32, 62: Art Resource, NY; pages 34, 41, 54, 59: Roland & Sabrina Michaud/Woodfin Camp & Associates; page 38: Christie's Images/ Bridgeman Art Library; page 39: Musée d'Art et d'Histoire, Geneva/Bridgeman Art Library; page 42: Werner Forman/Art Resource, NY; page 45: Victoria & Albert Museum, London/Bridgeman Art Library; page 47, 68: Robert Frerck/Woodfin Camp & Associates; page 49: Victoria & Albert Museum /Art Resource, NY; page 50: Private Collection/Bridgeman Art Library; pages 51, 56: Réunion des Musées Nationaux/Art Resource, NY; page 61: Wolfgang Kaehler/Corbis; page 63: Jeff Greenberg/The Image Works; page 66: Magdalen College, Oxford/Bridgeman Art Library; page 67: Erich Lessing/Art Resource, NY.

CONTENTS

CHAPTER ONE

FROM NOMADS TO SULTANS

The twentieth-century Turkish poet Nazim Hikmet once compared the shape of Anatolia to the head of a galloping horse charging westward out of the continent of Asia. The image is a fitting one considering the peninsula's long history of invasion and conquest by horse-mounted warriors.

The earliest Turks, the ancestors of the Ottoman Turks, lived in the steppes, or grasslands, of central Asia. This high, dry region stretches from north of Afghanistan and the Himalaya Mountains all the way to the northwestern part of China. Brief growing seasons, freezing winters, and scorching summers made agriculture extremely difficult. However, hardy breeds of cattle, sheep, and goats were able to survive in the treeless and wide-open expanse of the steppes. Given little choice as to livelihood, the Turks became herders.

Grazing exhausted the land, so once an area of the grasslands was eaten bare, the Turkish herders were forced to move their livestock. Over the years, a nomadic way of life evolved. The nomads continuously moved according to the needs of their animals, which in turn provided them with food and wool. Organization among the Turkish nomads was loose. They lived in separate tribes, with each tribe led by a respected male.

Disunited, the Turks posed little threat to other peoples. United, they were a formidable force. Sometimes they came together under one powerful leader, called a khan, for the purpose of raiding or conquest. Riding small, sturdy horses and armed only with bows, Turkish horsemen could easily launch a rapid, surprise attack against a foe and then just as quickly vanish. They used this tactic to raid areas of Europe and China. As they pressed into the lands bordering on the Middle East, they came into contact with Islam. This religion, founded by the prophet Muhammad in the

The Ottoman Turks had one of the mightiest armies in history. Under the leadership of Süleyman I in the 1500s, their empire dominated the eastern Mediterranean region. In this illustration from a medieval French manuscript, Turkish crossbowmen prepare to attack the island of Rhodes, in the Aegean Sea.

7

Arabian Peninsula in the 600s C.E.,* spread throughout the Middle East in the 700s. Contact with Islam would have great significance for the Turks.

The meeting ground for the Turks and Muslims—people who follow Islam—was Transoxiana, a region of central Asia that today is located within the borders of Uzbekistan. The people of Transoxiana had become Muslims in the 700s to 800s. Islam not only became their religion but also shaped their culture. Mosques were built for worship services, schools were set up to teach the religion, and government institutions were established to bring the Islamic legal tradition to all aspects of life. This way of life, centered around the worship of one God—who was called Allah in Arabic, the language of Muhammad—was profoundly different from that of the nomadic Turks.

Muslim missionaries in Transoxiana converted the Turkish tribes-people who moved into the region. Once most of the Turks of central Asia had been converted to Islam, they were accepted as important allies of the caliphs (KAY-lifs), the rulers of Muslim domains in the Middle East. Turkish warriors became soldiers in the armies of the caliphs. When the caliphs were weak, Turkish tribes managed to gather more and more power. One such group was the Seljuks, who established the first great Turkish empire.

The Seljuk Turks Enter Anatolia

The Seljuk Turks rose to prominence in the eleventh century in Transoxiana. Gradually they became so strong that they were able to seize lands on their borders. They moved into northeastern Persia in the mid-1000s and soon conquered all of that region. Tugrul, the Seljuks' leader, took the title of sultan, or "holder of power." At this point, the formerly nomadic Seljuks began to adopt a settled life, which included the administration of a government. Because they had no tradition of collecting taxes, organizing large fighting forces, or carrying out laws, the Seljuks adopted the methods of the former Muslim rulers of the lands they had conquered. They used those borrowed traditions to rule an

---

*Many systems of dating have been used by different cultures throughout history. This series of books uses B.C.E. (Before Common Era) and C.E. (Common Era) instead of B.C. (Before Christ) and A.D. (Anno Domini) out of respect for the diversity of the world's peoples.

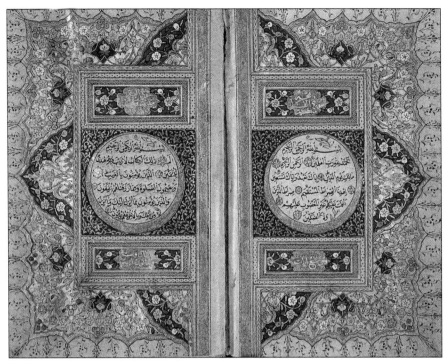

Two facing pages from the Koran, the holy book of Islam. The borders are filled with intricate paintings of flowers, and the circles in the center of each page contain passages from the Koran.

empire that soon stretched from central Asia through what are now Iraq and Iran and included the eastern half of Anatolia.

As their power grew, the Seljuks began to move into western Anatolia, where they came into contact with the peoples, armies, and institutions of the Byzantine Empire. The Byzantines, who were Eastern Orthodox Christians, had once controlled vast lands extending from the Caucasus Mountains in the east to the rim of northern Africa and as far west as Spain. By 1054, however, their empire had greatly shrunk in size. Byzantine lands south of Anatolia had been seized by Arab Muslim conquerors and absorbed into Islamic empires. Now the heartland of the Byzantine Empire was under pressure from the Seljuk Turks. In 1071, the Seljuk sultan Alp Arslan engaged the Byzantine army at Manzikert in eastern Anatolia and defeated it.

That victory opened Byzantine lands to Turkish settlement. With the Byzantine armies retreating in defeat and the empire in disarray, the

Seljuks were free to take Syria and Palestine unopposed. This period of conquest marked the height of Seljuk power.

In the late eleventh century, divisions began to grow within the Great Seljuk Empire. There were several reasons for this development. Following Turkish tribal traditions, Seljuk sultans divided their conquests among members of their families. Those family members were left free to rule their holdings and control their own armies. When a sultan died, it was common for a struggle to break out among his sons and nephews for control of the empire. This led to disunity. The traditional nomadic way of life of the Turkish tribes also contributed to the empire's problems. The independent nomad warriors who formed the core of the Seljuk armies and followed the sultan in conquering new lands were reluctant to give him their undivided allegiance. When the conquests were over, the nomads returned home to tend to their own interests.

By 1092, the Great Seljuk Empire had begun to break up. The Seljuks who had moved into Anatolia formed a separate empire called Seljuk Rum (for "Roman," as the Arabs called the Byzantine Empire). Four years later, in 1096, the Seljuks of Rum encountered the soldiers of

A nomad rests on his staff while his horse grazes. The army of the early Ottoman Turks was made up of nomad warriors.

the First Crusade—Europeans who invaded the Middle East in order to wrest control of the Holy Land from the Muslims. A long period of warfare and chaos followed. The first wave of crusaders defeated the Seljuks of Rum in battle. Sanjar, the last Great Seljuk sultan, tried unsuccessfully to restore the Seljuks' influence and territories. With his death in 1157, the period of Great Seljuk rule came to an end, though sultans would continue to rule in Seljuk Rum for another hundred years.

The Early Ottomans (1281–1446)

As the power of the Seljuk Turks began to decline, another nomadic Turkish people came into prominence in western Anatolia. These were the Ottoman Turks, whose name may have derived from their first leader, Osman I (ruled 1281–1326). The Ottomans settled in northwestern Anatolia early in the 1200s as vassals, or underlords, of the Seljuks of Rum. At this time, the Seljuks of Rum were being pressured by a foreign invader. The Mongols, another nomadic people from central Asia, were moving west in search of fresh pasturelands. Mongol tribes attacked Persia and established an empire there, then moved into Russia. By the 1200s, the Mongols had swept into central Anatolia and destroyed Seljuk Rum lands. They never established permanent settlements, however, and instead were content to take tribute from the people whose lands they invaded.

During the 1300s, various Ottoman sultans expanded their control over Seljuk-Mongol areas in Anatolia. Osman I was a skilled soldier and leader who brought many nomad groups under his banner to wage successful wars on other principalities in Anatolia. Making treaties when it suited him and playing one group against another, he gained more and more power and influence.

Osman was aided in his conquests by *ghazis* (GAH-zees)—Muslim "warriors of the faith" from the border areas of Anatolia who volunteered to take part in jihads (jih-HAHDS), or "holy wars." In its purest, most basic sense, *jihad* means the internal, spiritual struggle to become a better Muslim. It also has another meaning: the duty of a Muslim to advance Islam among nonbelievers and to defend the faith against its enemies.

During Osman's rule, the *ghazis* waged war against the Byzantine-Christian lands around them. In 1302, Osman defeated the Byzantines at

Sultan Osman I, in a seventeenth-century Turkish miniature painting. Osman was the founder and first sultan of the Ottoman Empire.

Nicaea (modern-day Iznik) and established an Ottoman principality. Thus Osman and his *ghazi* followers were the founders of the Ottoman state.

The Ottomans set up villages in the conquered Byzantine and Seljuk Rum lands in Anatolia. They began to impose taxes for the support of their young state. They also were ever eager to acquire new territories. That goal brought them into Europe. In 1352, Ottoman forces under the sultan Orhan crossed the Bosporus—one of the narrow straits that separates the continents of Europe and Asia— and established a presence on European soil. In 1354, they settled at Gallipoli, a peninsula that juts into the Aegean Sea. In 1361, they seized the city of Adrianople, in Thrace, renaming it Edirne. This city became the Ottoman center of power. Soon all of the former Byzantine lands around the city of Constantinople (modern-day Istanbul) were under their control. Then they advanced northwest into the Balkan Peninsula.

The peoples of the Balkans were separated from one another by steep mountain ranges and deep valleys. Each region was ruled by its own king or prince. These rulers frequently battled one another, and they often sided with the Ottomans in war if the end result suited their goals. Rather than attempting to conquer this divided region, the Ottomans decided on another tactic. When they defeated a Balkan king, they offered to allow him to keep his titles and lands in return for allegiance and support in time of war. One group that accepted this arrangement was the Serbs, who came under Ottoman rule in 1386. A few years later, however, the Serbs asserted their independence in a series of skirmishes and battles against the Ottomans.

In 1389, the Ottoman sultan Murat I faced the rebellious Serbs under their leader Prince Lazar and his Bosnian and Bulgarian allies. The two armies gathered at Kosovo Field—the "field of blackbirds"—on June 15. Just before the battle, Murat was assassinated by a Serb posing as a deserter. Murat's son,

Bayezit, took command and, in the battle that unfolded, led the Ottoman forces in a total defeat of the Serbs. The Ottomans captured Lazar and put him to death. Soon Serbian opposition to Ottoman control was broken. Sultan Bayezit I (nicknamed the Thunderbolt) continued the Turkish conquests in Europe and subdued Bulgaria. By 1400, the Ottoman Turks held lands that stretched from the Black to the Aegean Seas.

The Classical Age (1447–1566)

The city of Constantinople—all that was left of the once mighty Byzantine Empire—remained out of Ottoman reach. Whoever conquered it (and many had tried) would gain the prestige of controlling the most important city in the world: the point where Europe and Asia met, a port city once famed for its riches and trade in luxury items, and a seat of ancient imperial power. When Mehmet II (called the Conqueror) became sultan in 1451, he made it his goal to take Constantinople. Mehmet planned well. The Ottoman fleet was assembled and dropped anchor near the city walls. Continuing an Ottoman tradition known as *devsirme* (DEV-shur-mee), or "gathered," Mehmet had drafted young Christian boys from the Balkans, converted them to Islam, and trained them into a crack military corps called the Janissaries. The sultan added the Janissaries to his army of nearly 160,000. While the Byzantines sought help from the pope and European princes, the Ottoman grip around Constantinople gradually tightened.

In 1453, Mehmet began a fifty-four day siege of Constantinople. He used every means available to break through the ancient walls of the well-fortified city. The sultan commissioned a German engineer named Urban to create a huge cannon capable of smashing holes through the walls. Thirty pairs of oxen were used to haul the twenty-seven-foot-long cannon overland to within range of Constantinople. Once in position, it joined with other cannon in a bombardment that began on April 6. As the walls were damaged, the defenders quickly repaired them.

Earlier, in anticipation of an Ottoman invasion by sea, the Byzantines had placed a huge chain across the entrance to the Golden Horn, the harbor of Constantinople. Mehmet countered by building a road on which ships were maneuvered by means of tracks, over a hill to the edge of the Golden Horn. There, to the amazement of the Byzantines,

In 1453, the Byzantine city of Constantinople fell to the Ottoman Turks. Here Mehmet the Conqueror enters the city at the head of his victorious troops.

the ships were lowered into the harbor. On May 28, outgunned, outnumbered, and running dangerously short of food, the remaining eight thousand defenders of Constantinople gathered at Hagia Sophia, the great church of the Byzantine Empire, for a final prayer. Emperor Constantine XI joined the throng, said his prayers, and, as darkness enveloped the city, left the church to inspect the battered walls. On May 29, 1453, as the Ottomans finally broke through the walls of the city, Constantine himself forged forward to join in the hand-to-hand battle. He and the other defenders of Constantinople went to their deaths as the Ottoman soldiers overwhelmed them.

Mehmet's conquest of Constantinople brought the Byzantine Empire to a close. The Turks turned Hagia Sophia into a mosque, a Muslim house of worship. The city's other churches as well as its palaces and public buildings were protected and preserved for the sultan's use.

Over the next twenty years, Mehmet seized the Dardanelles, a thin waterway between Asia and Europe, and Ottoman ships sailed through the strait into the vast Mediterranean. The merchant empire of Venice dominated the Mediterranean's coasts and trade. From 1463 to 1479, the Ottomans battled the Venetians on land and sea, while Mehmet seized their goods and imprisoned their merchants. Ottoman Turkish armies also advanced into the Balkans and brought Bosnia into the sultan's empire. Mehmet demanded that all territories surrounding the Black Sea recognize Ottoman control. The Ottomans now ruled over two lands— Europe and Asia. Mehmet could truly call himself "Sovereign of the Two Lands and of the Two Seas."

The city of Istanbul, as viewed from its harbor, the Golden Horn, in the 1800s. The large buildings with domes and minarets (slender towers) are mosques, Muslim places of worship. The smaller buildings on the waterfront show the style of house favored by the city's Ottoman residents.

Mehmet the Conqueror regarded himself as the direct successor to the Byzantine emperors. Giving Constantinople a new name, Istanbul, he made it the capital of his empire. Mehmet rebuilt the city with mosques and Islamic religious schools called *medreses*. The sultan also had a vast palace called Topkapi built for himself and his court. And, since a city without people is nothing, he encouraged Muslims, Christians, and Jews to settle in Istanbul. Mehmet was keenly aware of the fact that he now ruled over an empire that was more than 50 percent Christian—including the peoples of former Byzantine lands and the Balkans—and took steps to gain their allegiance. With this in mind, he proclaimed himself the protector of the Christian Church in the Ottoman Empire.

The Decline of the Ottoman Empire (1567–1789)

The most outstanding leaders of the Ottoman Empire were the warrior-sultans including Mehmet II and two rulers of the early 1500s, Selim I and his son Süleyman I. They were able to build a huge empire through a combination of military conquests and capable rule. The reign of the most skilled of them, Süleyman I, marked the high point of Ottoman greatness.

The sultans who came after Süleyman were less able rulers. Some were incompetent or wasted the empire's resources satisfying their own lavish habits. Some gave up much of their authority to their chief adviser, the grand vizier. This arrangement worked well if the grand vizier was honest and capable. If he was not, the empire suffered.

Sultans were often involved in bloody struggles with family members to retain their power or dictate the succession. At first, any of the sons of a sultan could succeed to the throne. This was a tradition that dated back to the early Turkish and Mongol khans. Regardless of his methods, the son who gained power was usually looked upon as the legitimate ruler. There were problems with this system, however. Whenever a sultan died or was about to die, contests for power broke out among his sons. Sometimes these contests became full-fledged wars in which brothers killed brothers and fathers had their sons killed or imprisoned. The office of the Ottoman sultan was ultimately weakened as a result of these practices.

Other problems began to eat away at Ottoman power. One of these was linked to the Janissaries, the sultan's special fighting force. The Janissaries' role was to protect the life of the sultan, an assignment that

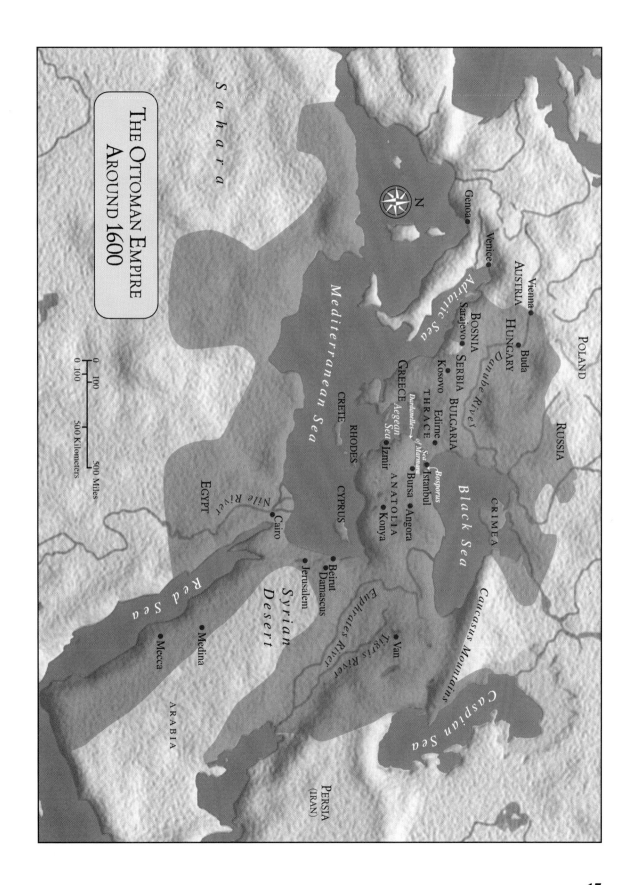

THE OTTOMAN EMPIRE
AROUND 1600

Sahara

N

Genoa

Venice

AUSTRIA

Vienna

Buda

HUNGARY

POLAND

Sarajevo

BOSNIA

Adriatic Sea

Danube River

RUSSIA

SERBIA

Kosovo

BULGARIA

Mediterranean Sea

CRETE

GREECE

Edirne

THRACE

Dardanelles

Aegean
Sea

Sea of Marmara

Bosporus

Istanbul

Izmir

Black Sea

CRIMEA

RHODES

Bursa

Angora

ANATOLIA

Konya

CYPRUS

Caucasus Mountains

EGYPT

Nile River

Cairo

Beirut

Damascus

Jerusalem

Euphrates River

Tigris River

Van

Red Sea

Syrian
Desert

Medina

Mecca

ARABIA

Caspian Sea

PERSIA
(IRAN)

0   100
0   100   500 Kilometers

500 Miles

17

made them very powerful indeed. They used their unique position to gain influence in the government. By the 1500s, the Janissaries had become so powerful that they were often able to overthrow a weak sultan or grand vizier and replace him with one of their favorites. When their influence was threatened, they rose up in revolt.

Other challenges came from forces outside the empire. The Europeans matched the Ottomans' military presence whenever and wherever they could. In the 1600s, Austrian and Polish forces drove the Ottomans from lands south of the Danube River. In the 1700s, Russia expelled them from the Crimea, the European peninsula that extends into the Black Sea.

There were economic challenges as well. At first, the Ottomans

The Battle of Lepanto: a famous naval engagement that took place in 1571 between the Ottoman Turks and the Austrians, with their allies from Spain, Venice, and Genoa. The Turks were defeated and their fleet destroyed.

encouraged trade with other nations as a way of building alliances and keeping would-be rivals, such as the Venetians, at peace. They welcomed English, French, and Dutch merchants and granted capitulations—agreements giving the foreigners the right to carry on trade within the empire. In return, the empire placed a customs tax on the trade. For a time, this arrangement benefited all parties. A steady supply of manufactured goods flowed into the empire, and the treasury filled with money from the customs taxes. The Europeans gained a large market for their ever-growing range of goods. However, when the Industrial Revolution began in Europe in the late 1700s, the nations of western Europe began to fiercely compete with one another for control over markets for their new factory-produced goods. They also began to take advantage of their trade agreements with the Ottomans. By the 1800s, inexpensive European goods were flooding into the eastern Mediterranean and pushing out native manufactures. Native products and producers were harmed as the empire became more and more dependent upon foreign imports.

Attitudes toward technological advances and scientific inquiry also harmed the Ottoman Empire. At various times, fanatical religious thinkers opposed innovations of all kinds, including the teaching of the sciences, claiming that inquiry was not in keeping with Islamic tradition. This began to change in the 1800s, when the Ottomans started to adopt European technology and ways of doing things. As the empire grew more efficient, it became evident to reformers that much work remained to be done. But the Ottoman Empire could not match Europe's industrial might nor compete with it militarily. All the Ottomans could do was try to improve on all fronts in a piecemeal fashion. That proved to be an impossible task.

The "Sick Man of Europe"

During the 1800s, non-Muslim groups throughout the Ottoman Empire were stirred by feelings of nationalism. They began to rediscover the legends and myths of their peoples and to write poems and books about the greatness of their pre-Ottoman past. Supported by the leaders of European nations, nationalist leaders began to demand separation from Ottoman rule.

The Balkans posed a special problem for the Ottomans. This region of southeastern Europe had long attracted the attention of Russia, the empire's chief rival to the north. Since the Ottoman conquest of the Byzantines in 1453, Russia had regarded itself as the leader of the Eastern

THE SULTAN AND THE TULIP

During the reign of Ahmet III (1703–1730), the Ottoman Empire began to slowly open up to the West. Ahmet's grand vizier, Ibrahim Pasha, sent a special envoy to the factories and workshops of France to learn about their technologies, with the aim of applying them to the Ottoman world. One of the results of these contacts was the introduction of the first printing press to the empire, in 1727. The Ottomans' first printed books were dictionaries and science texts. This time in Ottoman history also saw the introduction of Western-style palaces for the sultan and his court. These palaces were often surrounded by beautiful gardens filled with flowers. The most popular flower was the tulip.

Ahmet was fascinated by the tulip, which had already become an object of desire, even mania, in the Netherlands. The flower had been carried to the Netherlands from Turkey in the 1550s. For centuries before then, it had grown wild in central Asia, the ancestral home of the Turks. Ahmet spent untold amounts of money importing tulip bulbs. He had his gardeners carefully plant each flower bed with only one type of bulb. The sultan also organized festivals in honor of the tulip. The most extravagant celebration took place in April during the blooming period. Candles in lamps of different colors were hung throughout the gardens to illuminate the delicate blooms, while music played and poets recited. The sultan's love of the tulip earned him the name the "Tulip King" and the time of his reign the "Tulip Period."

Ahmet's love of flowers, poetry, and music was not shared by all. In 1730, the Janissaries rioted in Istanbul. They were angered by the sultan's extravagance and his grand vizier's inattention to military matters. They burned down Ahmet's French-style palace and forced him to surrender the throne in favor of his nephew. The sultan died in prison six years later. With his death, one of the most interesting periods in Ottoman history came to a sad close.

Orthodox Church and "big brother" to Orthodox Christians in southeastern Europe. When Christian separatist leaders in the Balkans began demanding independence from Ottoman-Islamic rule, the Russians believed it was their duty to aid them and help them drive out the

Muslims. Throughout the 1800s, several of the Balkan states—Greece, Serbia, Bulgaria, Romania, and Montenegro—fought for their freedom and won it.

Russia also had economic reasons for challenging the Ottomans. For years, Russia's merchant fleet had sought control of the warm waters around the Black Sea as well as the straits of the Bosporus and the Dardanelles. In the 1700s and 1800s, the Ottomans fought several wars to try to stop Russia's expansion into these territories. In the Crimean War (1853–1856), the Ottomans received help from France and Great Britain and held back the Russian advance. In another war with Russia, from 1877 to 1878, the empire suffered a terrible defeat—the loss of the northern and eastern shores of the Black Sea.

At home, Ottoman sultans went into debt to maintain the army and defend the empire. In the 1800s, the Ottoman Empire's deteriorating situation earned it the pathetic nickname of the "Sick Man of Europe."

A Greek soldier raises his flag over the bodies of defeated Turks, in this nineteenth-century painting. Greece won its independence from Ottoman rule in 1832.

Even in decline, the Ottoman Empire remained a functioning state whose people looked to it for leadership, justice, and services. The bureaucracy continued to carry out the day-to-day administration of the vast empire as young intellectuals tried to change the government from within. In 1895, they started a movement, the Committee of Union and Progress (CUP), to reform the government and make the empire democratic. Their goals included a written constitution and the establishment of an elected parliament. The leaders of the CUP eventually became known as the Young Turks. Their intended reforms promised a westernized military, an end to capitulations, and a new way of life for Turks similar to that of western Europeans. By the early 1900s, the Young Turks had become the most important force within the Ottoman government. However, the future they envisioned never came about. World War I interrupted their plans and devastated the empire.

The End of the Ottoman Empire

World War I was a turning point in the history of Europe and Turkey. The war broke out in August 1914 in Sarajevo, Bosnia. Great Britain, France, and Russia joined together as the Allies to fight Germany and Austria-Hungary, which formed the Central Powers. The Ottoman Empire reluctantly joined the Central Powers. It hoped to regain lost territory and protect itself from Russia, its longtime enemy. The decision to take part in the war had fatal consequences for the Turkish people.

In 1915, Turkish troops were fighting Russian forces in eastern Anatolia, a region historically inhabited by Armenians. The Armenians, who were Christian, had their own distinct, ancient culture and wanted their own nation. Armenian factions in and around the city of Van helped the Russian forces, viewing them as liberators from Ottoman rule. The Ottoman leaders, fearing a full-scale revolt by the Armenians and a breakdown of civil authority, ordered deportations. During the spring of 1915, about two million Armenians were forced to leave their homes in eastern Anatolia. The scene was grim. Eastern Anatolia was a devastated and disease-ridden war zone through which defeated Ottoman troops were retreating. Many of the Armenians trekking out of the area were attacked and killed by Turks and Kurds seeking revenge for Armenian atrocities. The survivors—mainly women and children—were marched to northern Syria. Altogether, about one million Armenians died during 1915. These events continue to haunt Armenian-Turkish relations.

Ottoman rule was under attack in the Middle East as well. The British drove the Ottoman forces out of Mesopotamia (present-day Iraq). In 1916, they helped the Arabs stage a revolt against Ottoman rule in Arabia and Syria.

By 1918, the Turkish troops were exhausted. About 325,000 Ottoman soldiers had been killed in the fighting and more than two million civilians throughout the empire had died. Millions of people were displaced. Muslims from the Balkans, the Crimea, and the Caucasus region were driven from their homes into Anatolia. With its government defeated and countless refugees pouring in, Turkey faced a desperate situation. The

The Battle of Gallipoli (1915) was one of the bloodiest fights of World War I. Here Australian troops struggle to move inland from their landing site on the beaches of the Gallipoli Peninsula. The Turkish troops prevented the Allies from capturing the peninsula and using it as a base to attack Istanbul.

government leaders fled into exile and the sultan asked for peace.

Greek, British, and French troops occupied Anatolia immediately after the war. Turkey's situation seemed hopeless as the victorious Allies prepared to carve it up. The terms of the Treaty of Sèvres, imposed upon the Ottoman sultan by the Allies in 1920, gave Greece western Anatolia and the Armenians their own country in eastern Anatolia. Arabs and Kurds were also promised their own territories. The Turks were to receive only a small area in central and northern Anatolia. In addition, Turkey was stripped of its former provinces of Mesopotamia, Palestine, Lebanon, and Syria. Peace seemed more terrible than defeat as the Turks faced the loss of the empire *and* their centuries-old homeland. Then, in 1919, one man made a decision that would have dramatic results for Turkey and its people. His name was Mustafa Kemal. Under his leadership, Turkey was reborn as a modern nation.

A New Nation is Born

Between 1919 and 1922, Mustafa Kemal, a former Ottoman army officer, led Turkish nationalist forces against the occupying army of Greece. Kemal had no organized army, few arms, and no money. Yet he set up his headquarters in Ankara and put together an army. The campaign he waged is known to Turks as the War for Independence. In 1922, Kemal abolished the office of the sultan and dissolved the Ottoman Empire.

Soon thereafter, a new peace treaty, the Treaty of Lausanne, was negotiated with the Allies. The treaty recognized the sovereignty and independence of Turkey and established its present-day borders. Its significance was great: Turkey was the only defeated nation in World War I to negotiate with the victors as an equal and influence the war's outcome.

Mustafa Kemal poses in the uniform of the Ottoman Army. Kemal was the defender of Gallipoli and earned the adoration of the Turkish people for his heroism. When the Republic of Turkey was declared in 1923, he became its first president.

HALIDE EDIB

Halide Edib was a famous Turkish writer, nationalist, and feminist whose life bridged the Ottoman Empire and the Republic of Turkey. Edib was born into a wealthy family in 1883 and educated at the American Women's College at Scutari. She was its first Turkish Muslim graduate and went on to teach at the University of Istanbul. Edib, who was married and had two children, was a daring woman for her time. She supported government reform and wrote on behalf of the Young Turk revolution of the early 1900s. Her main goals included the freeing of Turkish women from wearing the veil and education for young girls. Edib's articles on female emancipation angered many in Ottoman Turkey and she was forced to flee briefly. When her first husband took a second wife (legal under Ottoman law), she left him. This was an unusual act for a Muslim woman in the early 1900s.

In 1917, the Ottoman government assigned Edib the task of opening schools in Beirut and Damascus to replace foreign-run schools that had been closed as a result of World War I. She also operated an orphanage for Kurdish and Armenian children whose parents had been killed during the war. During Turkey's War for Independence, she supported the war effort and even served as a staff sergeant in the army of Mustafa Kemal. When the Republic of Turkey was established, Edib became its first minister of education.

Halide Edib died in 1964 after a long career as a teacher, reformer, and activist. She had witnessed the end of an empire and the birth of a new nation. Some of her most memorable works—short stories, plays, essays, and memoirs—were inspired by Turkey's struggle for independence and the changes brought about by westernization. One of her stories, *The Daughter of Smyrna,* deals with the rise of modern Turkey from the ruins of the Ottoman Empire.

On October 29, 1923, the Republic of Turkey was proclaimed and Mustafa Kemal was named its president. When the new president ordered all Turks to adopt Western-style last names in place of their traditional Ottoman names, the Turkish Grand National Assembly chose a name for him: Atatürk. The name means "Father Turk."

CHAPTER TWO

THE AGE OF SÜLEYMAN THE MAGNIFICENT

The Ottoman Empire reached its period of greatest power and glory during the reign of Mehmet II's great-grandson, Süleyman I, from 1520 to 1566. Known to Europeans as Süleyman the Magnificent because of the cultural richness and material wealth of his court, the sultan was also a brilliant general whose military exploits terrified his foes.

To his subjects, Süleyman was known as *kanuni,* or "Lawgiver," for his role in establishing Ottoman law codes to provide order and justice in the empire. He took existing Islamic sacred laws and combined them with common, everyday law to make one unified legal system. This system spelled out the rights and duties of the sultan and his subjects, how the government was organized, how different officials and their departments functioned, and what kinds of taxes were to be collected. The legal system guaranteed justice before the law and set up a system of fines for offenses. Süleyman's organization of the law made it clear that the sultan had total authority to make laws that governed the administration of the empire. In a letter to the king of France, Süleyman described himself as the "Sultan of Sultans, king of kings . . . God's shadow on earth, emperor and sovereign lord."

Under Süleyman's leadership, the Ottoman Empire enjoyed great wealth. The empire's merchants controlled the valuable coffee trade of Cairo, Egypt, as well as the caravan routes that crossed the Syrian and Sahara Deserts. Money from that trade flowed into the sultan's treasury in the form of taxes. Süleyman also established commercial ties with European nations. He allowed Europeans to settle in Istanbul and granted them the right to carry out trade there. The empire taxed that trade, too.

Sultan Süleyman I rides at the center of his troops during the Battle of Mohacs, in Hungary (1526). Süleyman is surrounded by the Janissaries, the sultan's special fighting force.

The sultan used his great wealth not only to wage war but also to support Turkish artisans, poets, and writers. Süleyman encouraged these people to create beautiful works of art for his court and for the many public buildings constructed under his patronage. Some of the arts that flourished during Süleyman's reign were calligraphy (the art of fine writing), tile making, textile making, and painting in miniature.

The Mosque of Süleyman

The beautification of the imperial city of Istanbul was one of Süleyman's goals during his long reign. His chief architect was Mimar Sinan. Born in the late 1490s, Sinan came from a Christian family and was drafted into the service of the sultan through the *devsirme*. He received training as an engineer in Süleyman's army and, like many *devsirme,* achieved a high position in the sultan's service. Sinan designed and built more than three hundred structures throughout the empire. These included public works such as baths, bridges, and aqueducts as well as elegant tombs and mosques. But Mimar Sinan's fame is the result of his masterpiece: the Süleymaniye, or Mosque of Süleyman, built between 1550 and 1557.

Located on a hill overlooking the Golden Horn, the Süleymaniye is Istanbul's largest mosque. Sinan had traveled widely and had seen many different kinds of buildings: Christian churches, ancient Greek and Roman ruins, Middle Eastern mosques. He used his observations of all these different architectural styles in preparing his structure. Intellectually and artistically challenged by Hagia Sophia, the famed Byzantine church whose massive dome dominated Istanbul's skyline, the architect aimed to match and improve upon this great Christian achievement, for the greater glory of Islam. The result was the Süleymaniye, a rectangular prayer hall covered by a large but graceful eighty-six-foot-wide central dome. Tiles in shades of turquoise, sapphire, and red, depicting flowers and trees, decorate the Süleymaniye's interior. Around the inside of the window-lit main dome, tiles form words from the Koran, the holy book of Islam: "God is the light of the heavens and the earth."

The imperial mosque was part of a *kulliye,* a walled complex of buildings (also designed by Sinan), each of which served a different religious or charitable function. Providing for the well-being of his subjects was one of a sultan's most important tasks. The buildings in the Süleymaniye

The Süleymaniye was built for Süleyman the Magnificent by his court architect, Sinan. The massive mosque, sitting on a hill overlooking the Bosporus and Golden Horn, can still be seen today.

complex included religious schools, a library for scholars, a hospital, an orphanage, a kitchen where the poor were fed at the expense of the sultan, public baths, and a caravanserai, or guest quarters for travelers.

CARAVANSERAIS

Caravanserais were guest quarters for caravans. Funded by contributions from the sultan and other well-to-do Ottomans, they were built at approximately twenty-five-mile intervals (the average daily traveling time for a caravan) throughout the empire. Caravans followed a timetable that allowed for rest stops. The trip from Izmir to Istanbul, for example, might take a week. Travelers started out at sunrise and continued until darkness approached; then it was time to rest. Another caravan might leave Istanbul for eastern Anatolia. This lengthy trip required many stops for the travelers and their animals.

A typical caravanserai was a large, walled building whose interior was one huge courtyard. Off the courtyard were many rooms. Traveling merchants slept in the rooms and rested and fed their pack animals (either camels or horses) in the courtyard. The merchants were given food for themselves and their animals for up to three days.

Caravanserais were sometimes built in towns and cities, but these were mainly used as selling places for merchants from a particular country. A city caravanserai might also be used as a place to sell a single commodity, such as spices or cloth.

The Palace of the Sultan

Topkapi Palace was the home of the Ottoman sultans from 1465 to 1856. During that time, it was the center of power in the empire. More than five thousand people lived in the palace during Süleyman's reign. Topkapi was actually several buildings, connected by courtyards and sprawling over a large area. The main buildings were the Outer Palace, the Inner Palace, and the Harem. The ideas of privacy and seclusion of the sultan from the public eye governed the palace's layout. Public business was conducted in the Outer Palace, while the sultan and his family lived in the Inner Palace and the Harem.

The Janissaries, the sultan's elite fighting force, stood on duty in a special courtyard on the palace grounds. The Court of the Divan served as the meeting place of the sultan's council of ministers. Other buildings included the Treasury, where tax money was stored; the Kitchens, ten large rooms where food for the palace residents was prepared; and the Palace School, the training ground for the empire's future soldiers, administrators, and bureaucrats. The entrance to the sultan's private living quarters, the Inner Palace, was called the Gate of Felicity. The sultan received his subjects there during specific times of the year. Inside the Gate of Felicity stood the Throne Room, where the sultan received ambassadors as well as the grand vizier and members of the Divan. Europeans called the entrance gate to the grand vizier's palace quarters the Sublime Porte and, in time, the Porte became the West's name for the whole Ottoman Empire.

The Harem, the dwelling place of the sultan's wives, mistresses, mother, and children, was the most private place within Topkapi. Like the

A caravan approaches a caravanserai—an inn for traders and their pack animals.

rest of the Ottoman court, the Harem had its own hierarchy, or classification based on each person's role or authority. The mother of the reigning sultan, called the *valide sultan,* was the most powerful individual in the Harem. From her high position, she ruled over the other women, all of whom vied with one another for power and influence with the sultan. The *valide sultan* often used her influence with her son to advance her favorites and dictate policy within the court. The "power behind the throne" was a term often used by court visitors when referring to the *valide sultan.*

A sultan's wife is entertained in the privacy of the Harem, the part of Topkapi Palace set aside for the family of the Ottoman ruler.

The *valide sultan* was followed in importance by the legal wives of the ruler—according to Islamic law, the sultan could have four wives. Then, in descending order of status, determined by their closeness to the sultan, came his favorite mistresses. These women had no rights under the law, because they were not legally wives. But if one of them had a son who became heir to the throne, her importance to the sultan and her influence in the Harem grew substantially.

A Training Ground for Leaders

Like the sultans before him, Süleyman provided for the education of the young. He increased the number of *medreses* in Istanbul and also built numerous colleges. In the *medreses,* boys learned to read and write and were taught about Islam. Some students went on to study at colleges, which were attached to the main mosques in the capital. Their course of study included grammar, philosophy, geometry, astronomy, and astrology (then considered a valid course of study). The most capable students continued their studies at schools of even higher learning. They became teachers or religious leaders.

The most prestigious school in the Ottoman Empire was the Palace School, founded by Mehmet the Conqueror and housed in Topkapi Palace. There young boys, many of them Christian youths gathered through the *devsirme,* studied to become public servants. Students attended the Palace School for fourteen years. Most graduates were assigned to military and government jobs throughout the empire. Many of the best students became pages to the sultan. The school was highly successful in training statesmen and leaders: four out of every five grand viziers graduated from the Palace School.

Poetry and Literature at Court

The Ottoman sultans loved poetry and many practiced writing verses. Süleyman the Magnificent wrote almost three thousand poems. Writers and poets were invited to live at the imperial court and provide the sultan and his courtiers with exquisite verses. Most Ottoman poetry was very romantic and dealt primarily with love, gardens, beautiful women, and the brave deeds of heroes. Poems were meant to be sung, accompanied by a stringed instrument such as a lute. Court poetry was written in Ottoman Turkish, a blend of Arabic, Turkish, and Persian words.

Most Ottoman poets also praised or memorialized the sultan, their main supporter. Baki, a poet and friend of Süleyman's, wrote the following lines upon learning of the sultan's death during a military campaign in Hungary in 1566:

In this detail from a Turkish miniature painting, a musician-poet plays a huge pear-shaped lute called an oud for the delight of the sultan and his court.

The master rider of the realm of bliss
For whose careering steed the field of the world was narrow . . .
He laid his face to the ground, graciously, like a fresh rose
  petal,
The treasurer of time put him in the coffer, like a jewel.

Trade and Commerce

The city of Istanbul was the world's hub of trade and commerce. Its commercial role had begun in ancient times, when the Greek-founded city was called Byzantium, and had continued in Byzantine times, when it was called Constantinople. Ships crossed the Black Sea from the southern coast of Russia to Istanbul, packed with grain, furs, timber, and amber. Caravans laden with silk, the most sought-after trade item before and during the time of Süleyman, traveled from China through Persia and Anatolia and then to Bursa, a city south of Istanbul. There the silk exchanged hands and was transferred to other caravans before arriving at Istanbul. The precious cloth was carried overland to cities such as Sarajevo, Vienna, Prague, Budapest, and Paris, where the rich would pay high prices for it. Ships from Venice and Genoa picked up trade goods in Istanbul and carried them out into the Mediterranean Sea and eventually to ports in Europe. The Ottomans placed a tax on every transaction made in this vast international trade. Those taxes became a source of incredible wealth for the empire.

Merchants in Istanbul also imported goods from around the empire for use by the city's inhabitants. These items included foods such as grain, cheese, salt, sugar, and spices, as well as materials needed by local craftsworkers and artisans. Gold came from Syria and Egypt, wood from the forests of eastern Anatolia.

The Ottoman government did much to promote trade and to protect those who took part in it. It prevented thieves from raiding caravans and set up caravanserais where weary traders could rest before continuing on to their destination. On the sea, the Ottoman navy policed ports and coastlines to keep pirates away from trading vessels. With the government providing security, the empire was a safe place to carry out trade.

The work of the craftsworkers, artisans, and merchants of the Ottoman Empire was organized and supervised by guilds. The craft guilds

CHRONICLER OF ISTANBUL

One of the liveliest writers of Ottoman times was Evliya Celebi. Born in Istanbul in 1611, Evliya came from an upper-class family. His family sent him to school, where he studied languages, music, grammar, calligraphy, and the Koran, which he excelled in singing and reading. Evliya's education prepared him well for a career at the sultan's court, but he was a dreamy young man and wanted a different kind of life. In the introduction to his multivolume work *Seyahatname,* or "Book of Travels," Evliya described his leanings.

> *It was during the . . . reign of Murat IV that I first began to wander in the gardens around Istanbul and to think of extensive travels, hoping thus to escape from the power of my father, mother, and brethren. . . . When I heard a description of the . . . four corners of the world, I became . . . anxious to see the world.*

At age twenty-one, Evliya decided to devote his life to studying history and the city of Istanbul. Descriptions of the city take up most of the Book of Travels. The rest of the work describes his forty years of wandering around the Ottoman Empire. During this time, Evliya claimed, he fought in more than twenty battles and visited eighteen countries. None of the places he visited seemed to compare to Istanbul, however. Here is an excerpt from Evliya's description of one of the major events in the city's history, the procession of the guilds ordered by Sultan Murat IV in 1638. The procession lasted for three days, and more than seven hundred guilds passed in review before the people of the city.

> *All these guilds pass in wagons or on foot, with the instruments of their handicraft, and are busy with great noise at their work. The Carpenters prepare wooden houses, the Builders raise walls, the Woodcutters pass with loads of trees, the Sawyers pass sawing them, the Masons whiten their shops, the Chalk-Makers crunch chalk and whiten their faces, playing a thousand tricks. . . . The Toy-Makers . . . exhibit on wagons a thousand trifles and toys for children to play with. . . . The Bakers pass working at their trade, some baking and throwing small loaves among the crowd.*

Evliya Celebi died in 1682. His images of Istanbul are among the most famous and lasting descriptions of life in the Ottoman capital during the seventeenth century.

were responsible for training workers through the master and apprentice system and for establishing a level of quality for all goods produced by guild members. While there were women in the many different crafts and trades, working in separate rooms or behind curtains in their husbands' or fathers' workshops, women were not allowed to join the guilds.

When dealing with the government, each guild sent its leader—a person chosen by the masters—to speak for the guild members. The government in turn sent out inspectors to examine the marketplaces in Istanbul and other cities throughout the empire to make sure no one was charging more than the government-set price for an item.

The most famous marketplace in Istanbul was the Grand Bazaar, a network of streets and shops covered by a roof and contained within its own walls. Construction of the Grand Bazaar had begun under Mehmet the Conqueror, and it originally included only a few warehouses in which merchants and craftspeople worked and kept their goods. In a short time, merchants representing different trades began to set up their stalls around the warehouses. Soon alleyways spread out in various directions. Caravans stopped nearby and unloaded their goods for quick trading. Over the years, the complex became so large and attracted so many merchants that it had to be protected by a gate, which was locked at night to protect the wares. Eventually, the whole structure was covered over with a vaulted roof.

City Life

The people of Istanbul lived in neighborhoods, or districts. Each district was a self-contained place with its own mosque (or church or synagogue, if the residents were non-Muslims), public fountain, shops, public bath, and private homes. The homes were usually two- or three-story wooden houses. Wood was plentiful in Ottoman times and was brought to the city from the forests along the Black Sea and from the Balkans.

A well-to-do Istanbul family might live mainly on the upper floors of a house, while the servants used the street-level floor for cooking and storing food. One or several rooms on the upper floors projected out over the street. Shutters on the numerous doors and windows gave privacy and closed out the winter winds. In summer, the shutters were thrown open to allow breezes to flow through the house. Poor families lived in houses

The Grand Bazaar in Istanbul was one of the world's great marketplaces. Customers could find spices, jewels, carpets, silks, objects made of gold and ivory, and other luxury items.

that were similarly constructed but had fewer levels and rooms.

The most desirable kind of house in Istanbul was the *yali*, a large structure situated on the banks of the Bosporus. Like most houses in the city, the *yali* was made of wood and sometimes decorated with carvings. It had doors and windows that opened out to receive the breezes coming off the water. The very rich often increased the size of their *yalis* to include gardens and walkways.

Whether grand or humble, Ottoman houses usually provided separate rooms for the women. Wealthy Muslim women were secluded, eating their meals and entertaining themselves in their own quarters. Seclusion was a sign of their special status and proof that their families were able to provide them with a life of ease and privacy. Their work was done by servants, so they were not usually seen by outsiders, except in rare instances. Poor or working-class women were more visible to the outside world as they went about their work inside and outside their homes, shopped, and raised their children.

City dwellers worked hard but also enjoyed life. After long hours of work, people of all ranks took their relaxation at public baths, or *hammans*. The largest *hammans* had several rooms. One was a warm, high-ceilinged room in which people steamed. Other rooms were set aside for washing or for splashing in a central pool. The heat in the steaming room came from fires kept burning underneath the tile floor. People sat on marble benches built against the walls. For well-to-do clients, there were private dressing rooms and baths. Working-class city women often had their own separate *hammans* where they, like their male counterparts, could relax, meet friends, and gossip. The *hammans* were so popular that people often brought food to eat and stayed for hours.

A woman and her slave at a hammam, *or Ottoman public bath. The woman's rich clothing, which includes a fur-trimmed coat, an embroidered brocade dress, and wide pants called* shalvar, *indicates that she is from the upper class. The elevated shoes were used for walking in muddy streets.*

CHAPTER THREE

THE TURKS AND ISLAM

Islam was the main religion in the Ottoman Empire. It came to Anatolia in the eleventh century when nomadic Turkish peoples brought the faith with them as they entered the peninsula. The nomads had been converted to Islam by Muslim preachers in central Asia. At the height of their power, the Ottoman Turks ruled the world's largest Muslim empire, extending from northern Africa to the Balkans. In Anatolia and elsewhere, Islam shaped Ottoman Turkish life in numerous ways—from art and architecture to dress to the way people thought and behaved.

Beliefs of Islam

Islam is not a religion that can be practiced by merely reciting prayers and carrying out rituals. It is a faith that encompasses all aspects of a person's day-to-day living.

Islam teaches belief in one God. The word *Muslim*—a follower of Islam—means "one who submits to God." According to Muslim beliefs, Allah (Arabic for "The God") revealed himself through the angel Gabriel to Muhammad, an Arab born around the year 570 in the city of Mecca, in the Arabian Peninsula. The people of Mecca were pagans at this time and worshipped many gods. Muhammad tried to convert them to belief in one God but failed. In 622, when enemies in Mecca plotted to murder Muhammad, he and his followers fled to the city of Medina, also in the Arabian Peninsula. Their migration, called the Hegira (*hijrah* in Arabic), is regarded by Muslims as the beginning of the first community in which Muslims governed themselves according to the new laws revealed to Muhammad by Allah.

By the time of Muhammad's death in 632, most people in the Arabian Peninsula had converted to Islam. Even Mecca came over to the new faith. In time, this city became the most important religious center in the Muslim world. A building in the center of Mecca, the Ka'ba, contained

A Muslim at prayer, as shown in an eighteenth-century Turkish miniature

numerous symbols of the gods worshipped by the pagan Arabs. When Mecca became a Muslim city, Muhammad cleared out all the pagan idols except for one, an ancient meteorite regarded by the pagan Arabs as representative of the Creator God of the Christians and Jews. He dedicated the Kaaba to God. Pilgrims came from far away to pray at the Kaaba, and in time, the pilgrimage to Mecca became one of the five pillars of Islam.

The plan of the Kaaba, in the holy city of Mecca, is part of this Turkish tile used to decorate a minbar, *or mosque pulpit.*

The Five Pillars of Islam

The five pillars, or main beliefs, of Islam are remarkable in their eloquent simplicity and straightforwardness. First and foremost is belief in one God and the role of Muhammad as his prophet. Muslims profess, or state, this belief when they say the words, "There is no God but God, and Muhammad is the messenger of God." These words, always spoken in Arabic, the language of Muhammad, are repeated during prayer.

The other main pillars of Islam are duties to be carried out by the faithful: prayer, giving alms to the poor and needy, fasting from sunrise to sunset each day during the month of Ramadan, and making the pilgrimage to Mecca at least once in one's life.

Muslims pray five times a day—at dawn, noon, midafternoon, dusk, and after dark—and follow a specific ritual at these times. By first standing, then bowing, then kneeling, and finally touching their foreheads to the ground, they show their submission to God. They perform their prayers while facing in the direction of the holy city of Mecca. Wherever they are, observant Muslims interrupt their activities at the prescribed time to remember God through the act of prayer. In addition to praying, Muslims must also give to the needy, with each person giving an amount in proportion to his or her wealth. A rich person should give more than a poor person, but all must give something.

The month of Ramadan (the ninth month of the Islamic calendar year) is a special time in Islam. It recalls the period when the Koran was first revealed to Muhammad. Ramadan is a chance for people to renew their spirit and affirm their belief in God. The practice of fasting reminds people what it is to be hungry, and it encourages them to be generous. Muslims are expected to fast every day during Ramadan. Nothing is supposed to pass a person's lips during the fast, not even water. The fast is broken each day at sunset. At the end of the month of Ramadan, when a new moon appears in the sky, Muslims celebrate by sharing meals, making visits to family and friends, and giving gifts to the poor.

The fifth pillar of Islam is the pilgrimage to Mecca. Each Muslim who is healthy and can afford to make the trip is expected to go to Mecca at least once in his or her life. Mecca is considered the most holy place in Islam, and pilgrims take part in special ceremonies there. They circle the Kaaba and pray. They also sacrifice an animal, usually a sheep or goat, to recall the Koran's story of God's acceptance of an animal as a sacrifice in place of Ismail, a son of Abraham. The sacrificed animal is cooked and the food is given to the needy. A person who makes the pilgrimage to

Musicians and flag bearers announce the end of Ramadan, the Muslim month of fasting.

THE KORAN, SACRED BOOK OF ISLAM

Muslims believe that the revelations of Allah to Muhammad are contained in the Koran. Many devout Muslims are able to recite suras, or chapters, of the Koran from memory. Written in rhymed prose, the Koran was the first great literary work of Islam. The first sura, called "The Opening," consists of seven lines. Nearly all Muslims know these words by heart.

In the name of Allah, Most Gracious, Most Merciful.
Praise be to Allah, the Cherisher and Sustainer of the Worlds;
Most Gracious, Most Merciful:
Master of the Day of Judgment.
You do we worship, and Your aid do we seek.
Show us the straight path.
The way of those on whom You have bestowed Your Grace,
  those whose portion is not wrath, and who do not go astray.

Islam and the Koran are both very specific about actions that comprise "going astray." These include murder, cheating, gambling, drinking alcohol, and eating pork. While a radical minority have twisted the words of the Koran to justify violence, the vast majority of Muslims believe that such actions go against the limits set by God and also harm the community of believers.

Mecca earns the right to be called by the title *hajji*. During the pilgrimage, devout Muslims also visit the city of Medina.

At the Mosque

Muslims can pray anywhere—at home, in an open field, at work. However, most Muslims go to a mosque to pray. Mosques can be found in cities, in rural towns and villages, on remote mountainsides, and at isolated crossroads. Many of the most famous and beautiful mosques in the Ottoman Empire were built in Istanbul, Edirne, and other cities.

Mosques are usually domed buildings with one or more slender towers called minarets at the corners. Today, as in Ottoman times, a man called a muezzin climbs up stairs inside the minaret to reach a small balcony at the top. From the balcony, he calls the faithful to prayer. In the largest cities and towns in the empire, each neighborhood had its own mosque. This is still true in present-day Turkey. Friday is the main Muslim day of worship, during which mosques fill with the faithful.

Before entering a mosque, worshippers must wash their hands, arms, face, and feet. An ornate fountain is located just outside the mosque for this purpose. Water is a powerful symbol in Islam, and the worshippers wash to purify their body in preparation for prayer. Washing also shows respect for God and for the human body, which was created by God. Men and women remove their shoes and leave them near the entrance to the mosque. To wear shoes inside would be an act of disrespect.

Once inside the mosque, men and women go to separate prayer places. Large city mosques built during the Ottoman period usually have the same layout: a rectangular structure formed by covered walkways opening inward to a central court. One of the sides of the court faces the holy city of Mecca and is decorated with a mihrab (MEE-reb), or pointed

The interior of a mosque, with worshippers at prayer. They are facing in the direction of the holy city of Mecca.

Sufism is a mystical form of Islam that rose up in Anatolia during the 1200s. Its name comes from the Arabic word *suf*, which means "wool." Early Sufis wore plain woolen clothes to show their devotion to a life of prayer and simplicity. Sufis attached themselves to teachers and organized themselves into brotherhoods. They wrote poetry and religious literature, made pilgrimages to Muslim holy places, and performed ritual exercises, such as dances and chants.

The most famous Sufi brotherhood today is the Mevlevi, known in the West as the Whirling Dervishes because of the ritual whirling dance they perform. Whirling is a sacred act to the Mevlevi Sufis. The white-clad brothers spin to music played on the *ney* (a flute), oud and *tanbur* (kinds of lutes), *kemenche* (violin), and percussion instruments. With arms outstretched, they spin with one palm raised up to heaven and the other facing the ground. Their wide bell-like skirts spread out as the brothers follow their special path. Their goal is to enter a prayerlike trance and, ultimately, receive the blessings of heaven.

The Mevlevi perform their ritual dance to the poetry of their founder and master, Mevlana (meaning "Our Master"). Mevlana's full name was Jalal al-Din Rumi (1207–1273). Rumi was a poet, writer, and teacher who composed many poems about Divine Love, the driving force behind a person's quest for Truth. His verses were meant to be sung by wandering minstrels. In that way, they became known to many people and were gradually absorbed into the culture of the Turks. Rumi also taught peace and tolerance for the beliefs of others. There were many approaches to knowing God, he said, and he respected the beliefs of Jews and Christians.

Rumi's poetry often expressed the indescribable, unknowable, all-

niche, in the wall. The faithful face the mihrab while they pray, using it to focus their minds. The mihrab may be covered with beautifully painted tiles and phrases from the Koran. Decorations in the form of intricate geometric patterns, curling vines, or ornate calligraphy sometimes cover the interior of the mihrab as well as the walls of the mosque.

Another feature of the mosque interior is the *minbar*, or pulpit. The imam, or Muslim prayer leader, stands on the stairs of the *minbar* to deliver a sermon during the worship service.

embracing nature of God and Divine Love. His mysticism is evident in the following excerpt.

The Unseen Power

We are the flute, our music is all Thine;
We are the mountains echoing only Thee;
And movest to defeat or victory;
Lions emblazoned high on flags unfurled—
Thy wind invisible sweeps us through the world.

Rumi lived most of his life in the Anatolian city of Konya. When he died, leaders of many different religions came to his funeral to honor a man who had shown respect for others and acted with compassion to all. Today his tomb in Konya, identified by its brilliant turquoise-tiled tower, is a site of Muslim pilgrimage.

Modern-day Mevlevi— followers of the thirteenth-century Sufi teacher and mystic Mevlana—perform their ritual whirling dance.

The earliest mosques were very simple and spare. During Ottoman times, however, they became major domed structures, as befitted the powerful sultans who commissioned them. Inside and out, Ottoman mosques were gorgeous, made so by the artisans who turned their labor into a form of worship. They covered the walls and floors with colored tiles, fitted windows with stained glass, and laid down beautiful woven carpets, all for the glorification of God.

CHAPTER FOUR

SHAPING THE EMPIRE

Like the Byzantine emperors before them, the Ottoman sultans were absolute rulers whose decrees were law. One word from the sultan and a humble person could be raised up or a mighty person cast down. The sultan was the commander in chief of the Ottoman army and navy. All positions in the Ottoman bureaucracy—the people who carried out the day-to-day tasks of governing—were filled by his authority. Answerable only to God, the sultan was also responsible for carrying out the *sharia,* a set of actions based on the Koran. According to the *sharia,* all actions are judged to be either required, commendable (praiseworthy), permitted, reprehensible (shameful), or forbidden.

Within the empire, the *sharia* was applied to every situation in which a legal decision had to be made. The judgments were handed down by the leading scholars of Islam, or muftis (MUF-teez), who were graduates of the most advanced *medreses* in the land. These scholars were part of the intellectual class of the Ottoman Empire. They wrote the law books, advised political leaders, and traveled throughout the empire interpreting the law and handing down opinions. All muftis were appointed by an elder, who was placed in his job by the sultan. The elder also named the judges of the courts throughout the empire. These judges were responsible for enforcing the laws of Islam and of the sultan. They were helped in this role by the governors appointed to carry out the sultan's commands in the provinces.

The Ottoman sultan was the defender of Islam's lands and the guardian of its holy places, including the cities of Mecca, Medina, and Jerusalem. He also controlled the main routes used by Muslim pilgrims on their way to the holy places.

At the Center, the Sultan

The Ottoman Empire was a highly centralized, militaristic state. At its center was the sultan. Radiating out from him were the members of the ruling class, who answered to the sultan and carried out his commands. They also collected the taxes and fought for the empire in times of war. In return, the sultan gave them wealth in the form of large estates.

Slavery was an important aspect of Ottoman society. Many of the military leaders and administrators in the empire were slaves. Some of these people had been captured from the armies of defeated foes and placed in the personal service of the sultan. Others were Christian Slavs who had been taken from their families in childhood as part of the *devsirme*. Raised as Muslims, they were taught the Turkish language and customs and trained to be soldiers and administrators, acting under the direct command of the sultan. These imperial slaves, who were also called

A sultan parades through Istanbul, surrounded by his Janissaries. Each person's rank in the elite corps is indicated by the elaborateness of his headgear and the richness of his garments.

A commander of the Janissaries, from an eighteenth-century engraving. The Janissaries, the personal guards of the sultan, had great power and influence at court.

devsirme, served as a counterbalance to the military ruling class, whose power and influence otherwise might threaten a sultan's control. Unlike slaves in other societies, the slaves of the sultan could rise through their own abilities. Many became rich and powerful, acted as advisers to their ruler, and even owned other slaves. Some joined the Janissaries, the sultan's elite private fighting force. No matter how high they rose, however, they remained slaves, and they could be deprived of their positions, wealth, and lives at the sultan's command.

The governed—the great mass of ordinary people—were at the outer rim of Ottoman society. They paid the taxes required by the sultan for the running of the state and were expected to be loyal to him. They took no part in the government—that was the role of the sultan and his officials. The sultan had obligations to the people, however, that could never be denied. He made sure that they were treated justly, according to the laws. He protected them against enemies and defended Islam, the religion of the empire. The teachings of Islam bound the sultans to practice charity. They did this in many ways, such as building mosques, food kitchens, and hospitals.

The sultan's work was carried out by a council of ministers called the Divan, named for the low sofas (divans) the ministers sat on when they met. The Divan received foreign ambassadors, drew up orders, looked into complaints, answered petitions, and decided on policy for the empire. The chief of the sultan's ministers was the grand vizier, who lived in a residence of his own at Topkapi Palace. He led the administration of the empire and the army and navy and answered directly to the sultan. Many grand viziers came from the *devsirme*.

One Empire, One Sultan, Many Peoples

By 1517, the Ottoman Turks had conquered Syria and Egypt. The addition of these lands to the empire gave them control over a network of ports and trade routes connecting Asia and Europe. The immense wealth that flowed through these ports and along these routes—textiles, fruit, exotic woods, metals, spices—was now under Ottoman control. The enlargement of the empire also meant that the sultan ruled over many different peoples, both Muslim and non-Muslim. These peoples made up the broad base of the empire. They were the merchants, farmers, and artisans who paid the taxes that supported the vast Ottoman state. Greeks, Armenians, Jews, Serbs, Bulgarians, and Romanians were some of the non-Muslims in the empire.

The Ottomans allowed non-Muslims to organize themselves in communities, each under its own religious head and with the right to govern itself. Non-Muslim communities—the Greek Orthodox community, the Armenian community, the Catholic community, the Jewish community, and so on– lived in their own neighborhoods and ran their own schools, churches or synagogues, and courts. They also took care of the welfare of

Jews were welcomed to the Ottoman Empire soon after the fall of Constantinople. This illustration shows the Hebrew Scriptures' Scroll of Esther and its case, decorated with silver, corals, and brocade.

51

A NATIONAL EPIC

Traditional beliefs in Ottoman society were handed down from generation to generation through storytelling. The first stories were myths and legends of the early nomadic tribes, which were recited by a poet to the accompaniment of music. These myths and legends were carried over the length and breadth of Anatolia by the Turks and were told over and over wherever people gathered. With each telling, the stories became richer and deeper in meaning.

One of the most important folktales in Turkish literature is *The Tales of Dede Korkut*. This long poem includes twelve separate but interrelated legends about the history of the early nomadic Turks. Dede Korkut was a legendary poet whose stories were first written down in the 1300s. One of his dramatic tales recounts the adventures of Bugach Khan, the only son of the leader Dirse Khan. Dirse's followers try to turn him against his son by planting false rumors about the young man. But when his father is captured by traitors, Bugach saves the older man's life. Because of his valor, Bugach is rewarded with a kingdom of his own.

In the following excerpt, Dede Korkut addresses Bugach's father after the boy has struggled with a bull and killed it.

O Dirse Khan!
Give this young man a principality now.
Give him a throne for the sake of his virtue.
Give him also a tall Bedouin horse
He can ride—such a capable man.
Give him ten thousand sheep
To make shish kebab for himself; he has virtue. . . .
Give a suit to this man and a coat that has birds on its
     shoulders.
Let him wear both of these; he has skill.
The young man fought and killed a bull on the playing field
     of Bayindir Khan,
Therefore, let your son's name be Bugach [Bull].
I give him his name, and may Allah give him his years of life.

their own people. Non-Muslims were free to practice their religion without persecution and to move about the empire unhindered. They also could rise within the ranks of Ottoman society. The Orthodox Christian patriarch and the chief rabbi of the Jewish community were ranking members of the Ottoman government.

The Ottomans considered ability more important than either birth or background. Many of the Jews in the Ottoman Empire had made their way east from Spain when that country expelled its Jewish population in 1492. In Ottoman lands, they found religious tolerance and the freedom to make a living. Many served as bankers to the central government or dealt in precious metals. Other non-Muslims dominated in different occupations. Greek merchants in Istanbul, for example, carried on the fur and grain trade across the Black Sea. Armenians took part in the silk trade with Persia and other lands to the east.

Ottoman subjects paid three kinds of taxes: taxes on crops, livestock, and fishing; taxes on imports, exports, manufactured goods, and goods sold in the city marketplaces; and a personal tax. This last tax was paid only by Christians and Jews, in return for the freedom to practice their religion without interference. Non-Muslims were exempt from serving in the military. Muslims paid no personal tax but had to serve in the military if and when they were needed.

Ottoman Cities and Towns

Ottoman life was centered in and around cities. Bustling cities and towns dominated trade, commerce, and government and attracted a wide variety of people. These population centers had the best schools and services, many kinds of available goods, and the best chances for improving one's fortunes. A multicultural mix of rich and poor people flowed in and out of the cities of the Ottoman Empire like the tide. Istanbul was one of the most fluid and cosmopolitan cities in the world. It grew and changed character over the centuries.

The major towns and cities in the Ottoman Empire were located along trade routes or near ports. They were centers of trade and government, where one could go to settle a dispute in front of a judge or to buy and sell goods in the markets. The largest towns had a garrison of soldiers, whose job was to protect the people of the town and its outlying areas,

The streets of Istanbul teemed with activity. Street entertainers included wild-animal tamers such as this man wrestling a bear.

which usually included villages within a day's walk from the town center.

In the late 1500s, Sarajevo (in modern-day Bosnia) was one of the most prosperous cities in the Ottoman Empire. It had more than one hundred mosques, a *tekke* (a lodge of the mystic Mevlevi sect), *hammans* (public baths), inns for travelers, a *serai* (governor's court), markets, libraries, and schools. It also had several bridges and a system of piped water.

Some of the buildings in Ottoman cities were outgrowths of the Islamic faith, which requires followers to practice charity. Buildings such as mosques, schools, and hospitals came into existence through the charitable contributions of rich and powerful Muslims. These people founded trusts for the carrying out of good works. Everyone—rich and poor alike—enjoyed the benefits of their charity, since it included the construction of public fountains, bridges, and roads.

City women, especially working-class women, had many opportunities for contact with the outside world. Wearing veils and long cloaks, in accordance with Islamic tradition and law, they left their homes to shop in the markets or visit the public baths. Upper-class women tended to have little contact with outsiders, however; their servants and slaves did their shopping and ran their errands for them. In the late 1800s and early 1900s, reforms in the Ottoman government gave women more freedom, including the right to attend new all-female schools.

In the Countryside

In contrast to life in the city, life in Ottoman villages and hamlets was quiet and tranquil, governed by tradition and the changing seasons. This

Ottoman women veiled themselves when they went out in public. These two women are buying sweets with their children at the Grand Bazaar.

Popular sports in the Ottoman countryside included wrestling, as shown in this Turkish miniature painting.

is where the vast number of people lived: the peasant farmers who made up the backbone of the empire, farmed the land, and paid most of the taxes.

Most villages and towns tended to look alike. Dirt roads led into a settlement of tightly clustered, flat-roofed houses made of sun-dried mud bricks, the cheapest and most plentiful material. In areas where timber was plentiful, houses were made out of wood. The simplest Ottoman farmhouse usually had no more than two or three rooms. One room was set aside for meeting and entertaining visitors. The other was for the family members. Prosperous farmers often lived in compounds consisting of a farmhouse and a nearby barn for animals. A courtyard united the buildings and a wall enclosed them all. In some regions, houses were built on two levels. The ground floor was used to house farm animals and store crops, while the family lived on the upper floor.

Furniture—tables, chairs, beds—was unknown to the early Ottomans and was not part of Ottoman tradition. Floors were covered by flat-woven carpets. Mattresses for sleeping were unrolled and spread out on the floor at night, rolled up and packed away during the day. The only seat was a low divan built into a wall, which might also be used as a sleeping platform at night.

There were very few services in the out-of-the-way villages. There might be a small store and, if the village was well-off, a primary school. Water came from a village well, which also served as a meeting place for the villagers. The mosque, with its dome and slender minaret, was the central point of each village. There might also be a church or synagogue. Non-Muslims lived in close proximity to Muslims in the villages and had daily contact with them.

In Ottoman society, the work was divided between men and women. The men clearly dominated, however. They made the decisions, spoke out in meetings, and did the heaviest labor on the farms. When not working, they gathered in the village tea- or coffeehouse to relax and share news. Each village was headed by a *muhtar,* or mayor. His role was to represent the village in contacts with the governor of the province. Women mainly worked in their homes, cooking, sewing, weaving, and raising their children. They also farmed the land with their husbands, helping to plant and harvest the crops.

Teaching the Young

In Ottoman villages, the responsibility for educating the young also was divided between men and women. The education of boys began in the home, where fathers and uncles taught them about farming. If the village had a school, boys might attend, mainly to learn about Islam. A well-to-do farmer might send his son to a more advanced school in a nearby town or city or have him tutored at home in various subjects.

Girls received very little formal education. They were expected to

IF YOU LIVED IN ISTANBUL

If you had been born in Istanbul during the reign of Süleyman the Magnificent, your way of life would have been determined by the facts of your birth—whether you were a boy or a girl, rich or poor, free or a slave—and also by your abilities. With this chart, you can trace the course your life might have taken as a well-to-do inhabitant of Istanbul in the 1500s.

You were born in Istanbul . . . .

As a Boy . . .   **As a Girl . . .**

You live with your parents, brothers, sisters, grandparents, uncles, and aunts in a wooden house in one of the city's many neighborhoods. Your mother and the family's servants and slaves take care of all your needs.

At age 7 you begin to study with a tutor, learning how to read and copy verses from the Koran. You may also learn arithmetic and grammar.

As a teenager you attend classes in a *medrese,* a school attached to one of the mosques in the city. Here you continue studying the Koran, as well as philosophy, some science, music, and poetry. Your father is a merchant, and it has been decided that you will become involved in his business. Before you are twenty, your family has found a wife for you and you are married.

As a young man you work hard learning your trade, buying and selling goods in Istanbul. You spend most of your time at your busy shop in the Grand Bazaar and also enjoy relaxing with friends at the public baths.

In your thirties and forties you live with your wife and five children in your own house. Your widowed mother and aunt and an unmarried sister live with you. Your role as a father is to teach your sons your trade, make sure they are educated, and help them make the connections that will serve them in their careers. You are the head of the family and are responsible for all who live under your roof.

At age 7 you spend all your time with your mother, sisters, aunts, and young cousins in the women's quarters of the house. You learn how to cook, sew, and run a household. The women also teach you prayers and how to read and write a little.

As a teenager you are old enough to marry and have children. Your father begins to talk to another family about matching you with their son. You are married in a celebration that lasts for several days. You move to your husband's house and live with his family.

As a wife and mother you care for your five children and supervise your household from your quarters in the harem. You sometimes help your husband in his business, but always in private. You use your influence to help your husband find good wives for your sons. When your husband dies in an epidemic that kills thousands of people in Istanbul, one of your sons takes you into his house. You never remarry.

When you die, your body is buried immediately, according to Muslim tradition. Men's graves in the cemetery are marked with a cylinder-shaped tombstone, engraved with a name and a stone turban indicating rank. Women's graves have a flat tombstone with a crown of flowers or fruit, and carved flowers to indicate how many children they had. Families and friends visit your grave and place offerings in a small basin dug in the center of the tombstone.

During Ottoman times, boys were educated at religious schools, where they learned to read and memorize the Koran. Here young boys are seated around their teacher.

marry and raise a family. Mothers and older sisters taught young girls the skills needed for running a household and taking care of the people in it. When a girl reached the age of twelve or thirteen, her family arranged a marriage for her. This is the way life was lived into the early 1900s.

In the cities, formal schooling was based on learning to read and write selections from the Koran. Young boys went to primary schools, where they learned about Islam and were taught to recite and copy selections from the holy book. Most educated people knew how to read and write some Arabic, the language of the Koran. As in the villages, few city girls attended schools. Only girls from the upper classes received any kind of formal education.

CHAPTER FIVE

THE OTTOMAN INFLUENCE LIVES ON

The modern nation of Turkey emerged from the remains of the Ottoman Empire in the first decades of the twentieth century, under the leadership of Kemal Atatürk. Like a finely cut gem, present-day Turkey reflects the numerous facets of both its location—on two continents—and its rich history. It is at once ancient and modern, forward-looking yet steeped in the Ottoman past.

The Ottoman Turks and the Seljuk Turks before them gave the nation of Turkey its name. They also gave it a language and culture. The earliest people to speak the Turkish language lived on the steppes of central Asia. These nomads traveled with their herds over a huge area that today includes western China, Siberia in Russia, and Kazakhstan, Turkmenistan, Kyrgyzstan, and other nations of the former Soviet Union. The Turks who migrated to Anatolia often shared the land with non-Turkish peoples such as Arabs, Jews, and Greeks. This multicultural mix was one of the dominant features of life in the Ottoman Empire.

In present-day Turkey, Turks make up about 80 to 88 percent of the population. There are many different people within this broad group, however. Some families reflect the ethnic mixing that went on during Ottoman times. For example, a Turkish boy or girl may have a Turkish grandmother, a Greek grandfather, and great-grandparents who came from Romania or the former Soviet republic of Georgia. Each ancestor brought his or her own language and customs to Turkey. All lived under Ottoman rule as subjects of the sultan.

A Tradition of Arts and Crafts

Unlike Westerners, who usually separated arts from crafts, the Ottoman

The interior of Istanbul's Grand Bazaar today. Our modern-day shopping malls were directly inspired by the Grand Bazaar.

Turks believed that there was no difference between the two. According to scholar and folklore expert Henry Glassie, "Any medium handled lovingly [could] become in Turkey a vehicle for art." Turkish artisans of Ottoman times carried on numerous traditional art forms. These included basket weaving, wood carving, ceramic making, and metalworking. In the hands of the artisan, each item expressed something about its creator. Many of the arts and crafts traditions practiced during the time of the Ottoman Empire survive to this day.

Woven Carpets

Few works of art combine beauty of form and practical function as completely as woven carpets. In Ottoman Turkey, the creation of carpets was a fine art as well as an ancient craft. It was essentially a woman's creation. While Turkish men herded their flocks of sheep and goats, the women spun the sheep's wool and goat hair to make yarn. From the yarn, they wove not only carpets, but also cloth to make such items as shawls

The colors and designs of this handwoven carpet indicate the region where it was made.

and scarves. The woven wool also went into the tents in which their families slept, the cushions and blankets on which they rested, and the saddlebags used to carry their belongings. They learned how to use special plants and tree bark to make colorful dyes for the yarn. The roots of an herb called madder root were used to make colors as varied as red, orange, pink, and purple. Saffron produced dyes of yellow and brown.

Since women were the weavers, they chose the designs, colors, and overall look of the carpets they created. Often their choices included scenes of everyday life. Carpets were filled with lively details such as animals, birds, flowers, and horsemen galloping after deer. Carpets had a practical purpose. For a nomadic people, they could be used as ground coverings for the inside of the family tent and then rolled up and folded when the time came to move to new pastures. The carpets were also a source of wealth for the family. In times of need, a family might sell a carpet or trade it for another item.

During the time of the Ottoman Empire, the sultans and other wealthy Turks sought the best and most beautiful carpets to use in their palaces or to present as gifts for a mosque. These carpets were often woven of silk instead of wool. Sometimes gold and silver threads were added. The floors of many of the most famous mosques in Ottoman Turkey were covered from wall to wall with carpets. The carpets of the sultans generally featured curving designs around a central motif called a medallion. Twenty-five feet long, the imperial carpets were large enough to fill a palace room. They became a treasured part of Ottoman art.

Creating a Carpet

During Ottoman times, carpets reflected the personal taste and vision of the individual weaver. Sometimes the weaver created the entire carpet herself, from spinning the yarn to the designing and weaving. Carpets with tree and flower designs were very popular, including roses, carnations, and tulips. Most carpets were trimmed with a fringe of knotted threads at each end. The knots in the fringe were a very important element of the design, since they told where the carpet came from. Double knots called Gordes knots were used by Turkish weavers, while single knots were used by Persian weavers. All the carpet's elements—its knots, designs, and colors—told the carpet's history. A carpet expert can "read" a carpet just like a book.

Ottoman Turkish artisans created many kinds of carpets. A kilim was a type of carpet made in eastern Turkey and central Asia. Unlike carpets with a velvetlike pile, kilims were flat-woven. They were used to cover floors, walls, and other surfaces. Kilim designs were often based on plants, trees, and animals. These designs were very old. A tree or plant with its branches outspread (the Tree of Life design) signified hope for life after death. A bird might symbolize many things: good luck, bad luck, happiness or joy, power or strength. An eye design protected against the "evil eye," or bad luck. A star expressed fertility. The colors of the kilim were bold and bright and often featured red, black, green, and gold. Kilims have been around for a very long time. Archaeologists have discovered remnants of kilims in the prehistoric mound of Catalhoyuk in Turkey, and the carpets are still made today.

In present-day Turkey, the art of the carpet weaver is protected. The government has started technical schools where young women can learn the historic designs and the skills needed to produce the best handwoven carpets. Some of these schools are in villages. City schools and universities

A Turkish woman weaves a carpet on a loom. It can take several months of painstaking work for a skilled weaver to complete a single carpet.

also teach the art of carpet weaving in an effort to preserve the past. At these schools, women learn how to use vegetable dyes and to re-create the traditional designs of their region. Some scholars of the art maintain that the best carpets are still the ones a woman makes for her own use, because each woman then puts a bit of herself into her creation.

Calligraphy—the Art of Fine Writing

Calligraphy is one of the most important arts of Turkey's Ottoman past and remains a distinctive art form in the present day. Its history is rooted in Islam. In the early years of Islam, Arab scribes created beautiful scripts, or styles of writing, which they used to copy down words and phrases from the Koran. They also created beautifully illuminated (decorated) Korans. These combined intricate script with pictures of animals and plants or geometric shapes.

The Ottoman Turks adopted the art of calligraphy from the Arabs and used it in many ways. One of their innovations was to use calligraphy to create intricate decorations for mosques and palaces as well as emblems for the sultan. The most important emblem was the sultan's *tugra,* or monogram. *Tugras* are still made for notable individuals such as the president of the Republic of Turkey.

Turkish calligraphers became the best in the Muslim world. Masters of calligraphy produced many different scripts. They trained for hours in imperial workshops. Sitting cross-legged, a calligrapher moved an inked reed pen across the page with one hand and balanced the paper with the other. The art of calligraphy is still practiced in Turkey, where it is taught by master calligraphers in their workshops and in religious schools. Like musicians, calligraphers do exercises to keep their hands strong and supple enough to control the many writing strokes required by their art.

Ceramics

In Turkish, the word *cini* means "tile." Over the centuries, *cini* has come to describe all white ceramic pottery painted with an underglaze of color. Turkish artisans often adopted and adapted ceramic forms from other cultures. A kind of pottery known as Iznik developed in Turkey around the 1400s. It was based on the famous blue-and-white porcelain favored

THE SULTAN'S MONOGRAM

The *tugra,* or monogram, of the sultan was the most visible piece of writing in the Ottoman Empire. It was used as the Grand Seal of the empire and appeared on every decree and important document. Each sultan's *tugra* was created especially for him by an artist called a *tugrakesh.* The artist used intricate lines to spell out the sultan's name, the name of his father, and other honorary titles such as "shah," "khan," and "the victorious." The *tugrakesh* tried to use a variety of details and colors to make each *tugra* unique. This became a challenge, since sultans might have several *tugras.* The most lavish of these were inked in gold paint and might depict lotus blossoms, palm leaves, swirling and twisting lines called arabesques, carnations, and clouds.

The tugra of Süleyman the Magnificent

by the rulers of China's Ming dynasty. The Ottoman sultans liked the porcelain so much that they became avid collectors. Transporting the delicate porcelain by caravan was expensive and difficult, so the sultans decided to establish a factory where Turkish potters could produce their own. The city of Iznik near the Sea of Marmara became the center of Turkish ceramics from the 1400s to the 1600s.

Iznik ceramics were made of white clay that was painted, glazed, and fired in an oven called a kiln. Ottoman artists soon elaborated on the traditional blue-and-white ware. By the 1500s, they were adding flowers, animals, and geometric patterns in colors such as green, red, yellow, and purple. Iznik ceramics caught the attention of Europeans, who began to copy it widely. They imitated the swirling motifs in a style that became known as *turquerie.*

The diverse output of Ottoman ceramic makers both instructs and inspires present-day Turkish artists. In ceramic workshops, artisans pick and choose details from masterpieces of the past. Then, using a time-honored technique, they stencil these designs in charcoal powder onto the plain white pottery. During this part of the process, the artist applies his or her own design elements. The next step is the application of the colors. Here the artist can choose from the shades of a specific time period or incorporate a set of colors from several eras. The final painted piece—a plate, vase, or bowl, for example—is then placed in the kiln, which fires the pottery and fixes the colors. After several days in the kiln, the finished piece is removed and allowed to cool.

An Isnik ceramic plate from the 1500s. The plate is decorated with tulips and carnations, two favorite flowers of the Ottoman Turks.

Miniature Paintings

The Ottoman sultans employed court painters to record and glorify their deeds in gorgeous miniature paintings. The practice of painting in miniature first appeared in Anatolia under the Seljuk Turks. In the fifteenth century, under Mehmet II, miniature painting became an important type of Ottoman art. It remained so during the reigns of succeeding sultans and reached a peak in the 1600s.

Miniature paintings portray individuals in a highly detailed style. In a portrait, the human figure is shown in profile or turned slightly toward the viewer. The expression on the face is usually serene. In group scenes, the faces of soldiers, courtiers, and others are indistinguishable, except

Sultan Mehmet II, as painted by the Italian artist Gentile Bellini. Bellini was called to Istanbul as a court painter in 1479 and painted this portrait of the sultan two years later, just before Mehmet's death.

for that of the sultan. Cityscapes and landscapes are flattened so that near and far objects appear to be the same size. Miniature paintings layer detail upon detail and use vivid colors that capture the eye of the viewer and draw it in. Battle scenes were a common subject of Ottoman painters, and so were images of the sultan hunting, listening to music, or even smelling a flower. The overall effect of the miniature is of an exquisitely rendered moment, frozen in time.

Miniatures were often created to illustrate books about a sultan's reign. One of the most outstanding of these is the *Süleymanname,* a book about Süleyman the Magnificent's conquests of the Balkans and Hungary. This work contains thirty-two miniatures showing castles, harbors, and cities as well as birds, animals, and trees. The colors used are blue, green, yellow, orange, red, and gold.

Portraits of sultans captured their character as well as their appearance. The most famous portraits of Mehmet the Conqueror were created by Italian artists brought to Istanbul to work for the sultan. In 1479, the Venetian painter Gentile Bellini arrived in Istanbul. His portrait of

SHADOW THEATER

Shadow theater is a famous folk art tradition in Turkey, where it grew up in the 1500s during the time of the Ottoman Empire.

In shadow theater, a puppet master moves a cutout, jointed figure behind a cloth screen, which is brightly lit from behind by an oil lamp. The fifteen-inch-high puppets are made of stiffened animal hide and painted with bright colors. They are moved around by means of attached sticks. Besides human characters, the puppets may include trees, ships, and monsters. Shadow theater usually requires two puppet masters, who each move two or more puppets at a time. The puppet masters also speak the voices of the characters and improvise sound effects. Music is provided by a small group of musicians who sit alongside the curtain. They introduce the performance with a fanfare and play musical themes for each character as it enters.

This puppet character, known as Crazyman, is used in the traditional Ottoman shadow theater, which is still popular in modern-day Turkey.

Turkish shadow theater is called Karagoz ("black eyes"), after its main character, a cunning street fellow. With his sidekick Hacivat, an educated person with a high self-regard, Karagoz has many adventures that poke fun at merchants, foreigners, and country folk. The stories sometimes involve demons, mythical animals, or fantasy creatures.

During the time of the Ottoman sultans, shadow theater was the only place where one might hear criticism of the government or of Ottoman society. Today puppet masters keep this traditional art form alive by performing in parks and theaters in Istanbul and other large towns and cities. There they combine the old stories with commentaries on present times.

Mehmet had great influence on Ottoman miniaturists. Another famous royal portrait shows Süleyman the Magnificent in his old age, an interesting and unconventional view. It was created by the Ottoman painter Haydar Reis, also known as Nigari, in the sixteenth century. Present-day Turkish artists paint in many different styles, but the influence of the Ottoman miniaturists, particularly their use of brilliant colors and their fascination with the details of everyday life, can still be seen in contemporary works.

Bridging Past and Present

Ottoman art was not limited to ceramics, calligraphy, and miniature painting. Artisans also created beautiful illuminations as frames for miniature paintings. Bookbinding was another important art form. The Koran and other books were bound in leather that was decorated with gold designs and embossed with floral or spiral patterns. The Ottomans' love of intricate display extended to their arms and armaments. Horsemen carried hand-tooled shields decorated with ivory inlay. Infantrymen, the foot soldiers of the sultan's army, wore handsome metal helmets covered with engraved designs. Wood carving also reached a high level of quality in the empire. Woodworkers created carved doors, shutters, and Koran holders and inlaid them with ivory, mother-of-pearl, and tortoiseshell. Ceilings in the homes of the wealthy were made of carved wood, too. *Minbars,* the pulpits in the mosques, demonstrated the wood-carver's art in a religious setting.

Today Turkish artisans continue many of the Ottoman era arts and crafts in workshops found in cities, towns, and villages. Some workshops are large enough to be called factories. Others are quite small. The smaller shops are usually family-run businesses with several generations working at the same craft under one roof. In this way, a master passes along his or her knowledge of Ottoman artistic traditions directly to a young apprentice. By fashioning beautiful works of art, present-day Turkish artisans are able to connect with the past and make a valuable contribution to the present.

The Ottoman Empire: A Time Line

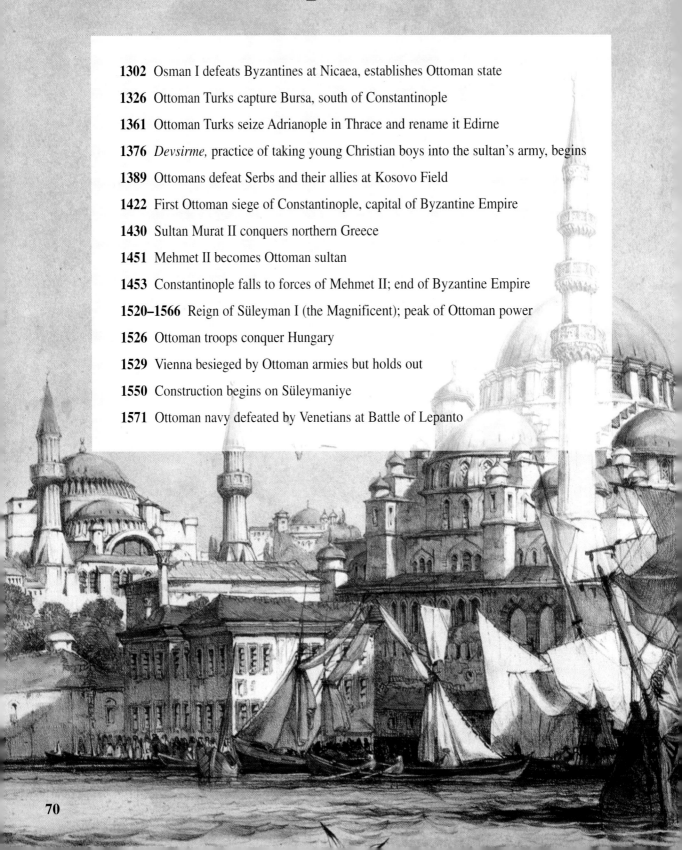

1302 Osman I defeats Byzantines at Nicaea, establishes Ottoman state

1326 Ottoman Turks capture Bursa, south of Constantinople

1361 Ottoman Turks seize Adrianople in Thrace and rename it Edirne

1376 *Devsirme,* practice of taking young Christian boys into the sultan's army, begins

1389 Ottomans defeat Serbs and their allies at Kosovo Field

1422 First Ottoman siege of Constantinople, capital of Byzantine Empire

1430 Sultan Murat II conquers northern Greece

1451 Mehmet II becomes Ottoman sultan

1453 Constantinople falls to forces of Mehmet II; end of Byzantine Empire

1520–1566 Reign of Süleyman I (the Magnificent); peak of Ottoman power

1526 Ottoman troops conquer Hungary

1529 Vienna besieged by Ottoman armies but holds out

1550 Construction begins on Süleymaniye

1571 Ottoman navy defeated by Venetians at Battle of Lepanto

1683 Ottoman siege of Vienna fails

1691–1695 Ottoman Empire at war with Poland, Austria, Russia, and Venice

1699 Ottomans sign Treaty of Karlowitz with European powers, give up lands in Europe

1703–1730 Tulip Period: introduction of first printing press in Istanbul and glorification of arts

1821 Greece revolts against Ottoman rule

1853–1856 Crimean War

1861–1876 Balkans rise up against Ottoman rule

1876 First Ottoman constitution allowed by sultan

1877 Russia declares war on Ottoman Empire

1878 Treaty of Berlin: Ottoman Empire loses lands in Balkans and northeastern Anatolia

1909 Young Turks force sultan to accept constitutional reforms

1914 Ottoman Empire enters World War I on side of Central Powers

1918 Ottoman Empire defeated in World War I

1919 Mustafa Kemal organizes resistance to Allied occupation of defeated Turkey

1922 Office of sultan abolished

1923 Republic of Turkey born

GLOSSARY

Anatolia: the large plateau that comprises the Asian part of Turkey

apprentice: a young person who learns a trade from an older, experienced worker

Bosporus: the twenty-mile-long strait that joins the Black Sea and the Sea of Marmara. The Bosporus divides the city of Istanbul in two.

Byzantine Empire: the Eastern Roman Empire, which became Christian under Emperor Constantine I, reached its peak in the 500s C.E., gradually declined, and was conquered by the Ottoman Turks in 1453

caliph (KAY-lif): the ruler of a Muslim domain

calligraphy: the art of fine handwriting

capitulations: agreements by which the Ottoman sultans granted trading privileges to foreigners. The first capitulations were granted by Süleyman I.

caravan: a company of people and their pack animals traveling in a group for safety. In Ottoman times, caravans transported trade goods overland.

caravanserai: a hostel (inn) for caravans

cini: a Turkish word meaning "tile"; it eventually came to mean a kind of glazed pottery

Dardanelles: the strait that connects the Sea of Marmara and the Aegean Sea

devsirme (DEV-shur-mee): a Turkish word meaning "gathered." The name was given to the Ottoman practice of taking young Christian boys into the service of the sultan, converting them to Islam, and training them to be soldiers or administrators; also the name of someone taken into the sultan's service in this way.

Divan: the Ottoman sultan's council of ministers

Eastern Orthodox Church: the Christian Church in the Byzantine Empire, the Balkans, and Russia, which split from the Western church in 1054

ghazis (GAH-zees): "warriors of the faith"; the early followers of Osman I who aided him in expanding his control over Anatolia in return for a share of the plunder

grand vizier: the Ottoman sultan's chief adviser

hammam: a public bath often found in Ottoman cities

Hegira: Muhammad's escape from Mecca to Medina in 622 C.E.; from the Arabic *hijrah,* or "flight"

imam: a Muslim prayer leader; an imam may also deliver a sermon in a mosque

Industrial Revolution: the rise of wide-scale manufacturing that took place in England and western Europe in the late 1700s and continued into the mid-1800s

Islam: the religion founded by Muhammad in the 600s C.E. and adopted by the Turks when they lived in central Asia; the main religion of the Ottoman Empire

Janissaries: the elite fighting force of the Ottoman sultan's army

kilim: a flat-woven carpet produced since prehistoric times in Anatolia and central Asia

kulliye: a complex of buildings built around a mosque, including schools, libraries, kitchens, and hospitals

Kurds: a people who lived in the eastern Anatolian part of the Ottoman Empire

medrese: an Islamic religious school

mihrab (MEE-reb): the prayer niche in a mosque; it denotes the direction of Mecca

minbar: the pulpit in a mosque

mosque: a Muslim house of worship

muezzin: a Muslim crier who calls the faithful to prayer

muftis (MUF-teez)**:** the leading legal scholars of Islam, who answer legal questions and, in so doing, help contribute to the Islamic legal tradition

nationalism: love of one's nation and devotion to its welfare

Ramadan: the ninth month of the Islamic calendar; a sacred time observed with fasting

Seljuk Turks: the first Turkish people to establish an empire in central and eastern Anatolia, in the 1000s

sharia: a set of actions based on the Koran; the basis for all legal decisions in the Ottoman Empire

sultan: one of the rulers of the Seljuk and Ottoman Turks; the word means "holder of power"

sura: a chapter of the Koran, the holy book of Islam

tribute: payment in the form of goods or flocks of animals

FOR FURTHER READING

Akurgal, Ekrem, ed. *The Art and Architecture of Turkey.* New York: Rizzoli, 1980.

Aslanapa, Oktay. *Turkish Art and Architecture.* New York: Praeger Publishers, 1971.

Atil, Esin. *Turkish Art.* Washington, D.C.: Smithsonian Institution Press, 1980.

Itzkowitz, Norman. *The Ottoman Empire and Islamic Tradition.* New York: Knopf, 1972.

Kinzer, Stephen. *Crescent and Star: Turkey between Two Worlds.* New York: Farrar, Straus and Giroux, 2001.

Kuran, Aptullah. *Sinan: The Grand Old Master of Ottoman Architecture.* Washington, D.C.: Institute of Turkish Studies, 1987.

Levey, Michael. *The World of Ottoman Art.* New York: Charles Scribner Sons, 1975.

Lewis, Bernard. *Istanbul and the Civilization of the Ottoman Empire.* Norman, OK: University of Oklahoma Press, 1963.

McDonagh, Bernard. *Blue Guide: Turkey.* New York: W. W. Norton, 1995.

Rice, David Talbot. *Constantinople from Byzantium to Istanbul.* New York: Stein and Day, 1965.

Rogers, J. M. *The Topkapi Saray Museum: The Treasury.* Boston: Little, Brown, 1987.

Shaw, Stanford, and Ezel Shaw. *History of the Ottoman Empire and Modern Turkey.* Vol. 1, *Empire of the Gazis: The Rise and Decline of the Ottoman Empire, 1280–1808.* New York: Cambridge University Press, 1976.

Video

Bauman, Susan, producer and director. *Süleyman the Magnificent.* Home Vision, 1987.

ON-LINE INFORMATION*

"Electric Library, Columbia Electronic Encyclopedia" at
  http://www.encyclopedia.com/articles/09702History.html
  Overview of Ottoman history

"Internet Modern History Sourcebook" at
  http://www.fordham.edu/halsall/mod/1908youngturk.html
  The Young Turks Proclamation for the Ottoman Empire, 1908

"Turkey in Pictures" at
  http://www.balsoy.com/Turkiye/inpictures/index.html
  Pictures of major Turkish cities and their important architectural
  sites

"World Civilizations" at
  http://www.wsu.edu:8080/~dee/OTTOMAN/OTTOMAN1.htm
  Overview of the Ottoman Empire and reign of Süleyman the
  Magnificent

*Websites change from time to time. For additional on-line information, check with the media
specialist at your local library.

BIBLIOGRAPHY

Arberry, A. J., ed. *Persian Poems, An Anthology of Verse Translations.* New York: Everyman's Library, 1972.

Freely, John. *Istanbul: The Imperial City.* New York: Viking, 1996.

Glassie, Henry. *Turkish Traditional Art Today.* Bloomington, IN: Indiana University Press, 1993.

Goodwin, Jason. *Lords of the Horizons: A History of the Ottoman Empire.* New York: Henry Holt, 1998.

Hambly, Gavin R. G., ed. *Women in the Medieval Islamic World.* New York: St. Martin's Press, 1998.

Heper, Metin. *Historical Dictionary of Turkey.* Metuchen, NJ: Scarecrow Press, 1994.

Inalcik, Halil. *The Ottoman Empire: The Classical Age, 1300–1600.* London: Phoenix Press, 1973.

Kinross, Lord. *The Ottoman Centuries: The Rise and Fall of the Turkish Empire.* New York: William Morrow, 1977.

Kritovoulos. *History of Mehmed the Conqueror.* Westport, CT: Greenwood Press, n.d.

Lapidus, Ira M. *A History of Islamic Societies.* Cambridge, MA: Cambridge University Press, 1988.

Lewis, Raphaela. *Everyday Life in Ottoman Turkey.* New York: Dorset Press, 1988.

Malcolm, Noel. *Bosnia: A Short History.* New York: New York University Press, 1994.

Mazower, Mark. *The Balkans: A Short History.* New York: Modern Library, 2000.

McCarthy, Justin. *The Ottoman Turks: An Introductory History to 1923.* New York: Addison Wesley Longman, 1997.

Menemencioglu, Nermin, ed. *The Penguin Book of Turkish Verse.* London: Penguin Books, 1978.

Norwich, John Julius. *Byzantium.* New York: Knopf, 1991.

Onger, Demir, et al. *Istanbul, Everyman Guides.* London: David Campbell, 1993.

Razwy, A. A., ed. *The Qur'an.* Translated by Abdullah Yusufali. Elmhurst, NY: Tahrike Tarsile Qur'an, n.d.

Robinson, Francis, ed. *Cambridge Illustrated History of the Islamic World.* Cambridge, MA: Cambridge University Press, 1996.

INDEX

Page numbers for illustrations are in boldface

ABOUT THE AUTHOR

Adriane Ruggiero writes nonfiction works with an emphasis on history, geography, and international affairs.

Her first book, *The Baltic Countries: Estonia, Latvia, and Lithuania,* was published in 1998 by Silver Burdett Press. Ms. Ruggiero is a contributor to several major reference works, including *The Dictionary of the Middle Ages, The Encyclopedia of Ancient Greece and Rome,* and *The International Dictionary of Modern Dance.* Her research often involves travel abroad. Adriane Ruggiero resides in Teaneck, New Jersey.